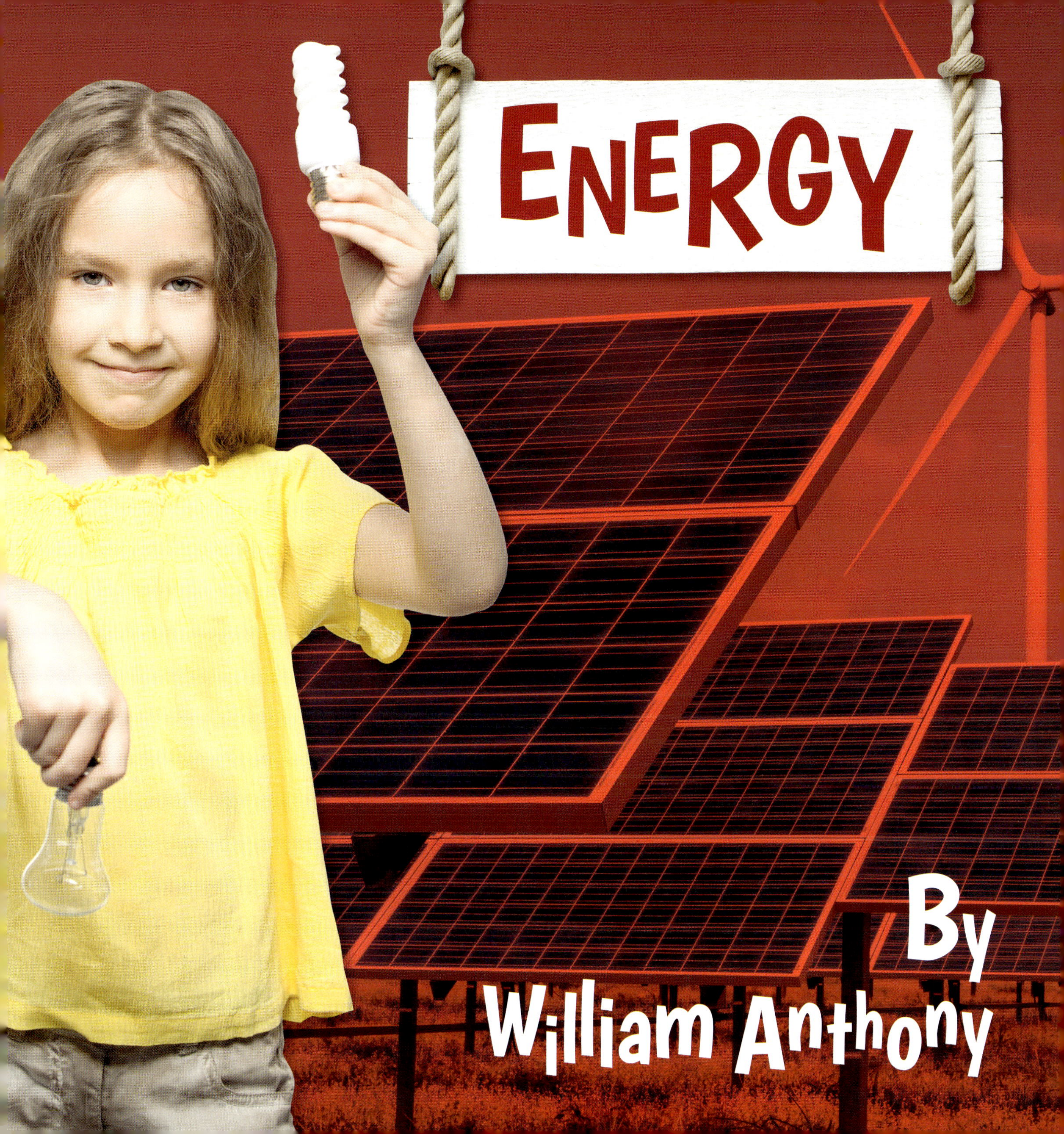
ENERGY
By
William Anthony

BookLife
PUBLISHING

©2019
BookLife Publishing Ltd.
King's Lynn
Norfolk PE30 4LS

Printed in Malaysia.

A catalogue record for this book is available from the British Library.

ISBN: 978-1-78637-563-6

Written by:
William Anthony

Edited by:
Holly Duhig

Designed by:
Gareth Liddington

Photocredits:

Cover - Soonthorn Wongsaita, Gladskikh Tatiana, Ruslan Ivantsov, Martin Lisner, Oyls, Tatyaby, 2 - Snova, 3 - udorn_1976, 4 - wavebreakmedia, 5 - Somchai Som, 6 - Africa Studio, J R Patterson, 7 - Africa Studio, LDprod, guteksk7, BATMANV, 8 - Rasta777, 9 - majeczka Sunny Forest, 10 - Koltsov Martin Capek, 11 - Morrowind, horiyan, 12 - PeterVrabel, Ensuper, Marian Weyo, 13 - DeVaul, 14 - Ugis Riba, Tim Bird, 15 - Anna Vaczi, 16 - Viacheslav Rubei, Wang An Qi, 17 - esbobeldijk, 18 - Blue Planet Studio, Mimadeo, 19 - Stockr, 20 - Breedfoto, 21 - Viliam.M, 22 - PopTika, Monkey Business Images.

Images are courtesy of Shutterstock.com. With thanks to Getty Images, Thinkstock Photo and iStockphoto.

CONTENTS

Page 4	What Is Energy?
Page 6	Types of Energy
Page 8	Making Energy
Page 10	Electricity
Page 12	Fossil Fuels
Page 14	Nuclear Power
Page 16	Solar Power
Page 18	Wind Power
Page 20	Hydropower
Page 22	Protect the Planet
Page 24	Glossary and Index

Words that look like this can be found in the glossary on page 24.

WHAT IS ENERGY?

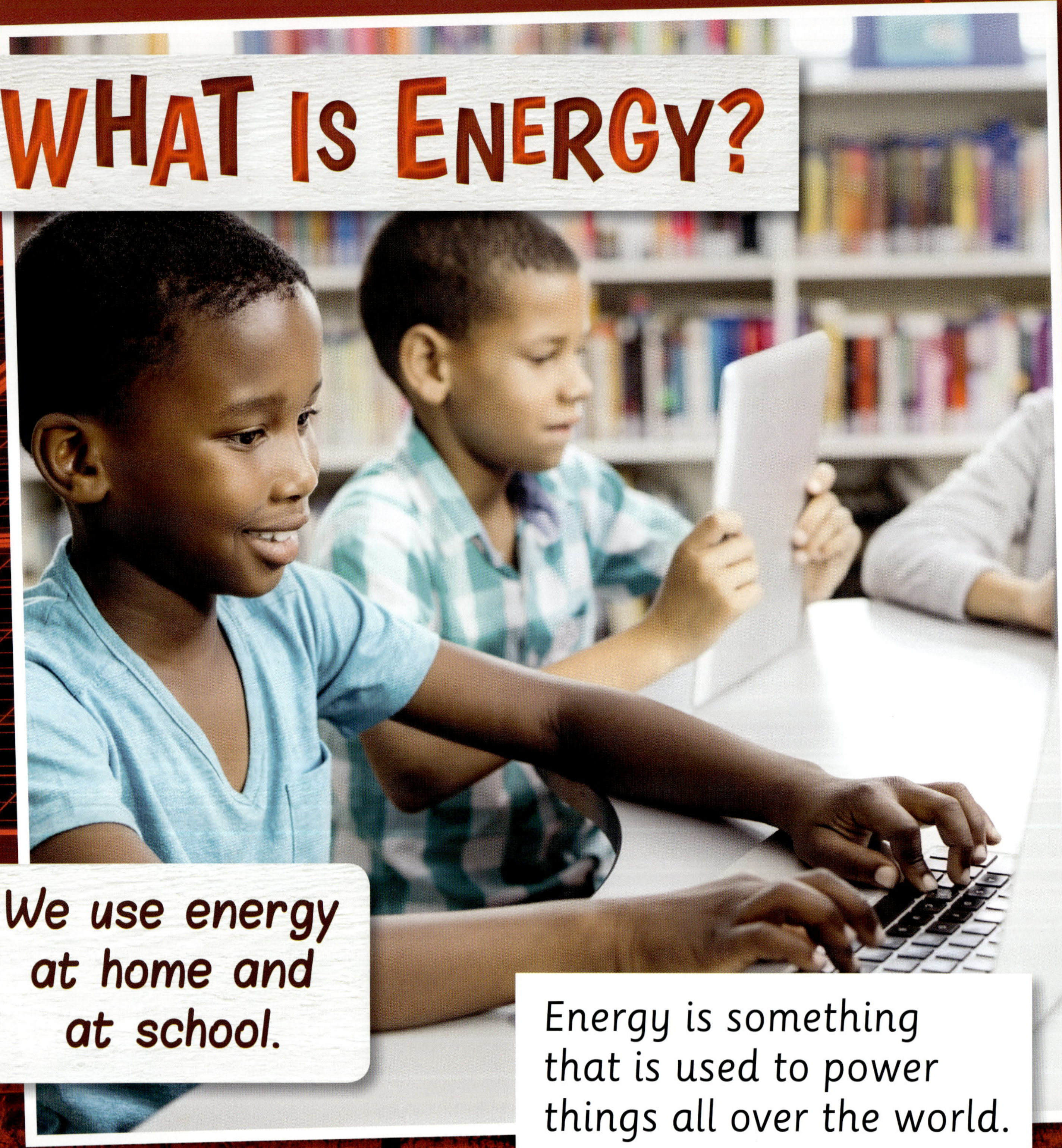

We use energy at home and at school.

Energy is something that is used to power things all over the world.

We can make things such as light, sound and heat using energy.

TYPES OF ENERGY

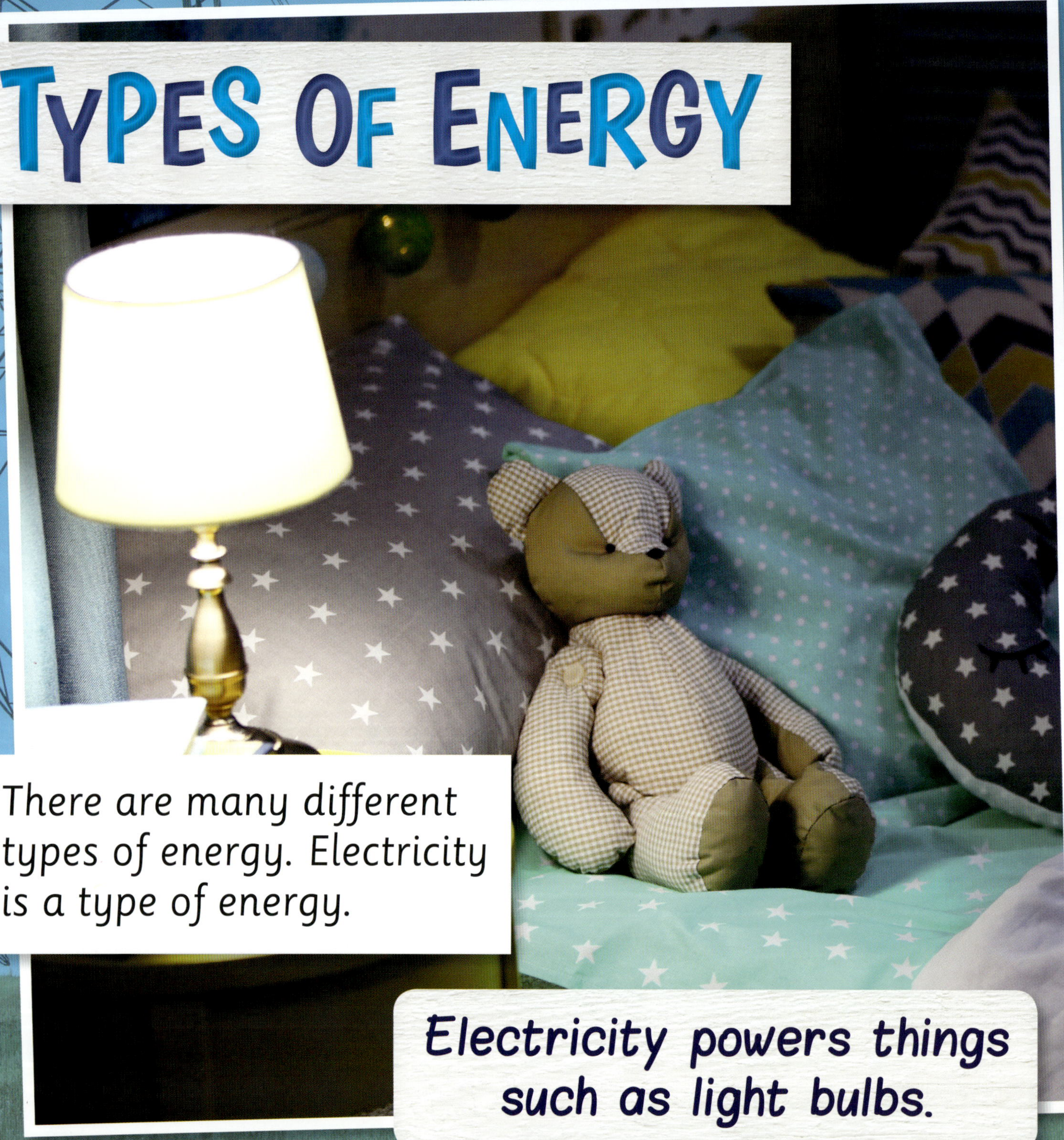

There are many different types of energy. Electricity is a type of energy.

Electricity powers things such as light bulbs.

These things all use electrical energy:

TELEVISION

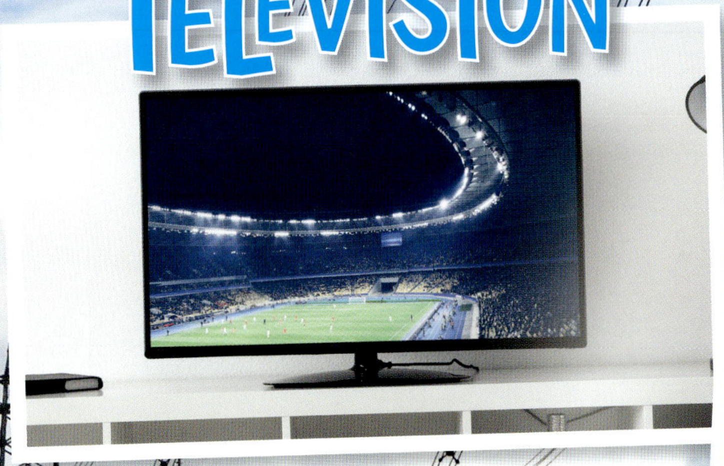

MOBILE PHONE

LAPTOP

MICROWAVE

MAKING ENERGY

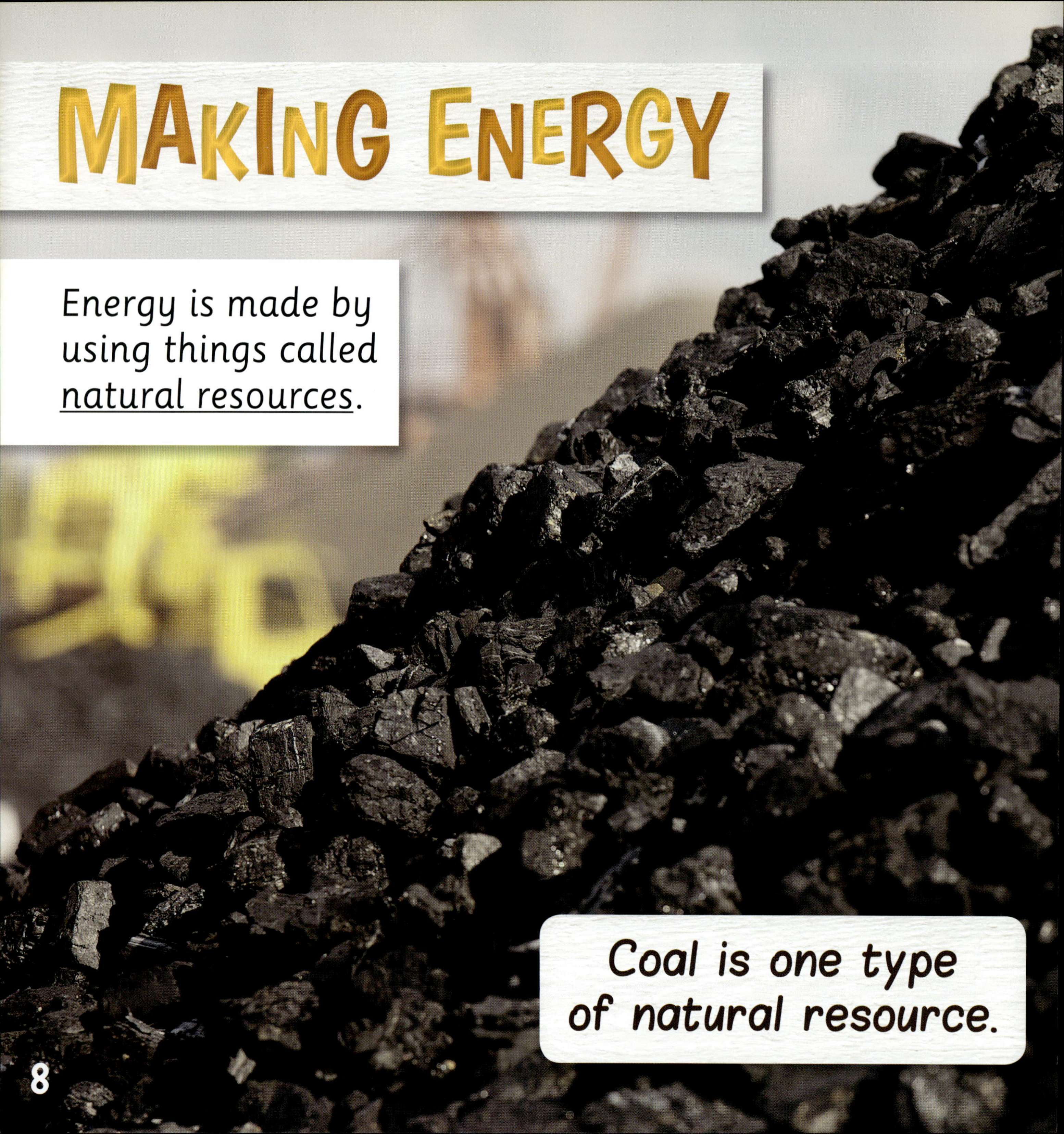

Energy is made by using things called natural resources.

Coal is one type of natural resource.

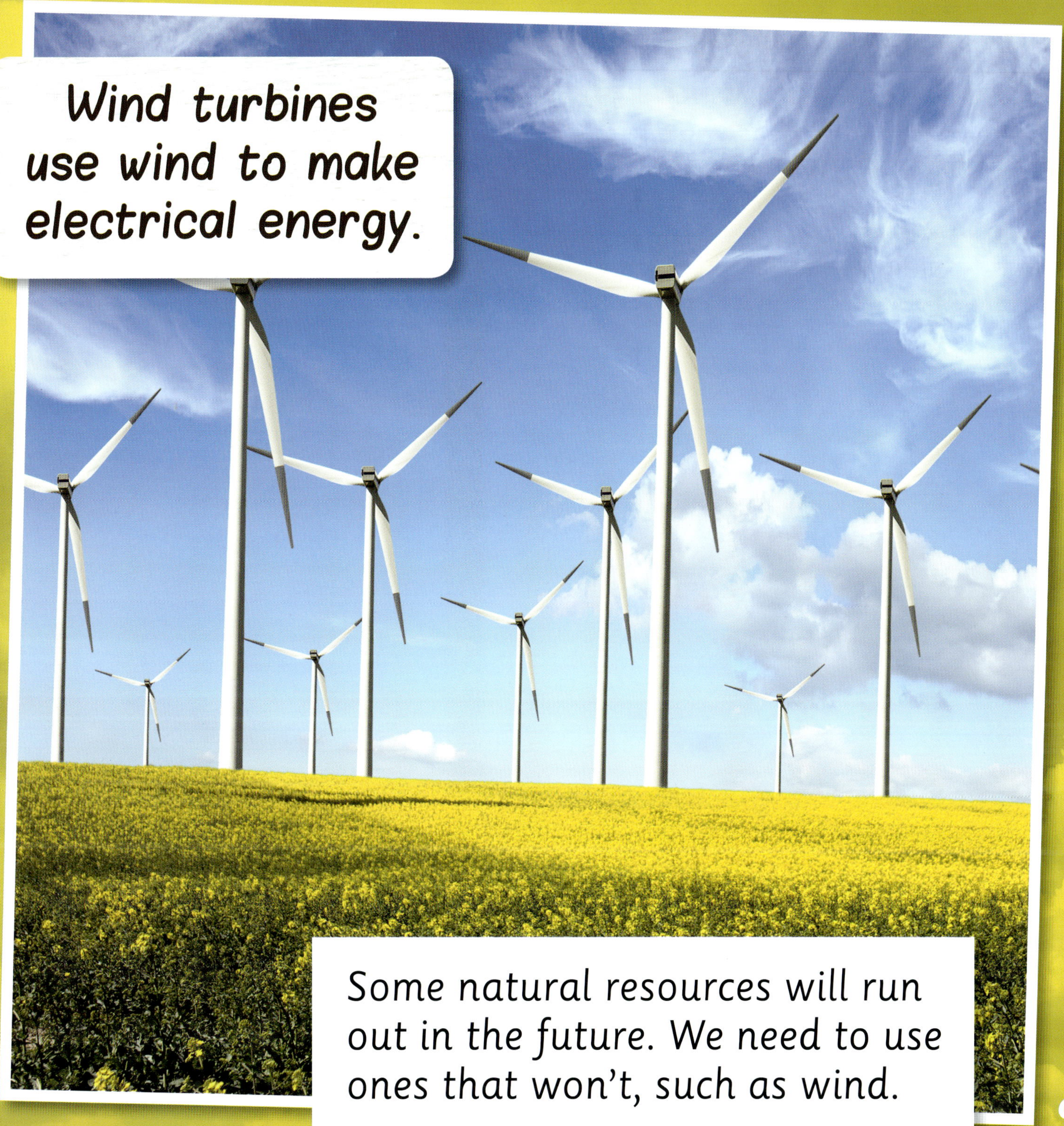

Wind turbines use wind to make electrical energy.

Some natural resources will run out in the future. We need to use ones that won't, such as wind.

ELECTRICITY

Electricity powers things in your home and school.

Can you name something in your home that uses electricity?

Electricity keeps your fridge running and makes your TV work.

Fossil Fuels

We can make electricity by burning coal, oil and gas. These are called fossil fuels.

Fossil fuels are natural resources.

Fossil fuels will run out if we keep using them. Burning them is also not good for the planet.

Burning fossil fuels can make the air dirty.

NUCLEAR POWER

We can make energy in a nuclear power station.

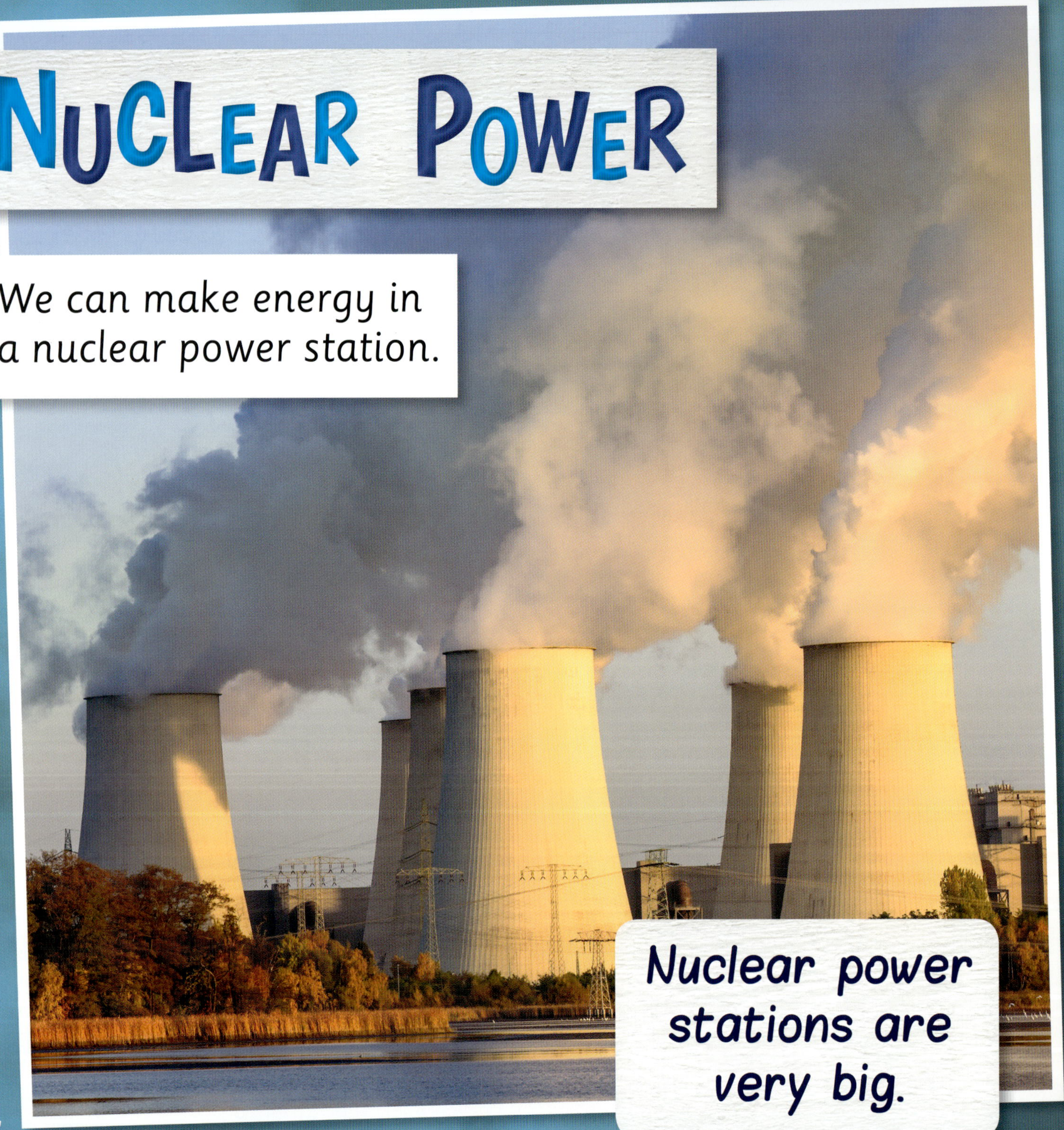

Nuclear power stations are very big.

Nuclear fuel will run out one day, too.

Some people think that it is a <u>risky</u> way to make energy.

SOLAR POWER

We can make power by using energy from the Sun! This is called solar power.

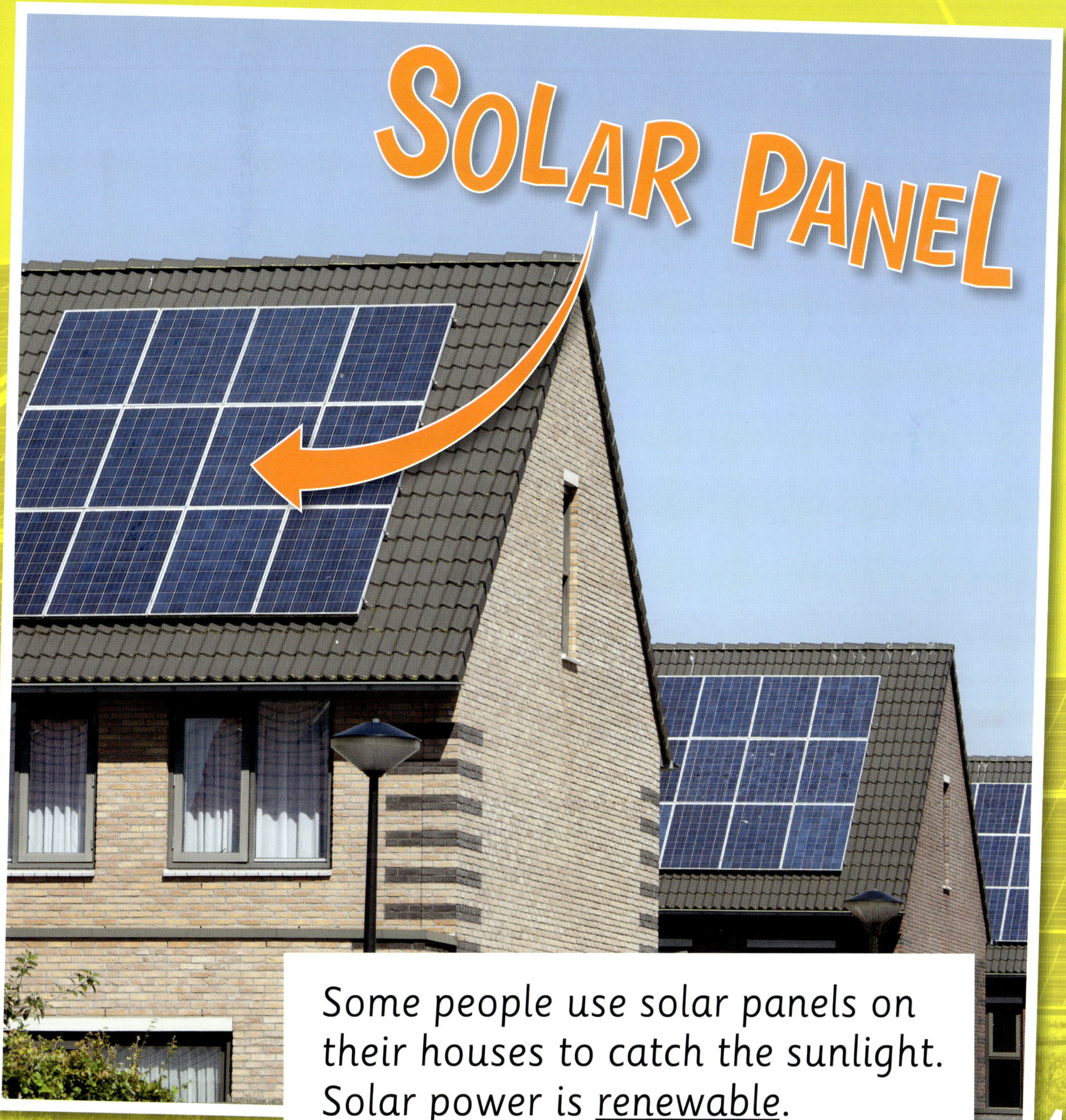

Some people use solar panels on their houses to catch the sunlight. Solar power is renewable.

WIND POWER

We can also use the wind to make energy. We use wind turbines for this.

Wind turbines look like huge fans!

The wind pushes the turbine round and makes it spin. This is what makes the energy.

We will never run out of wind!

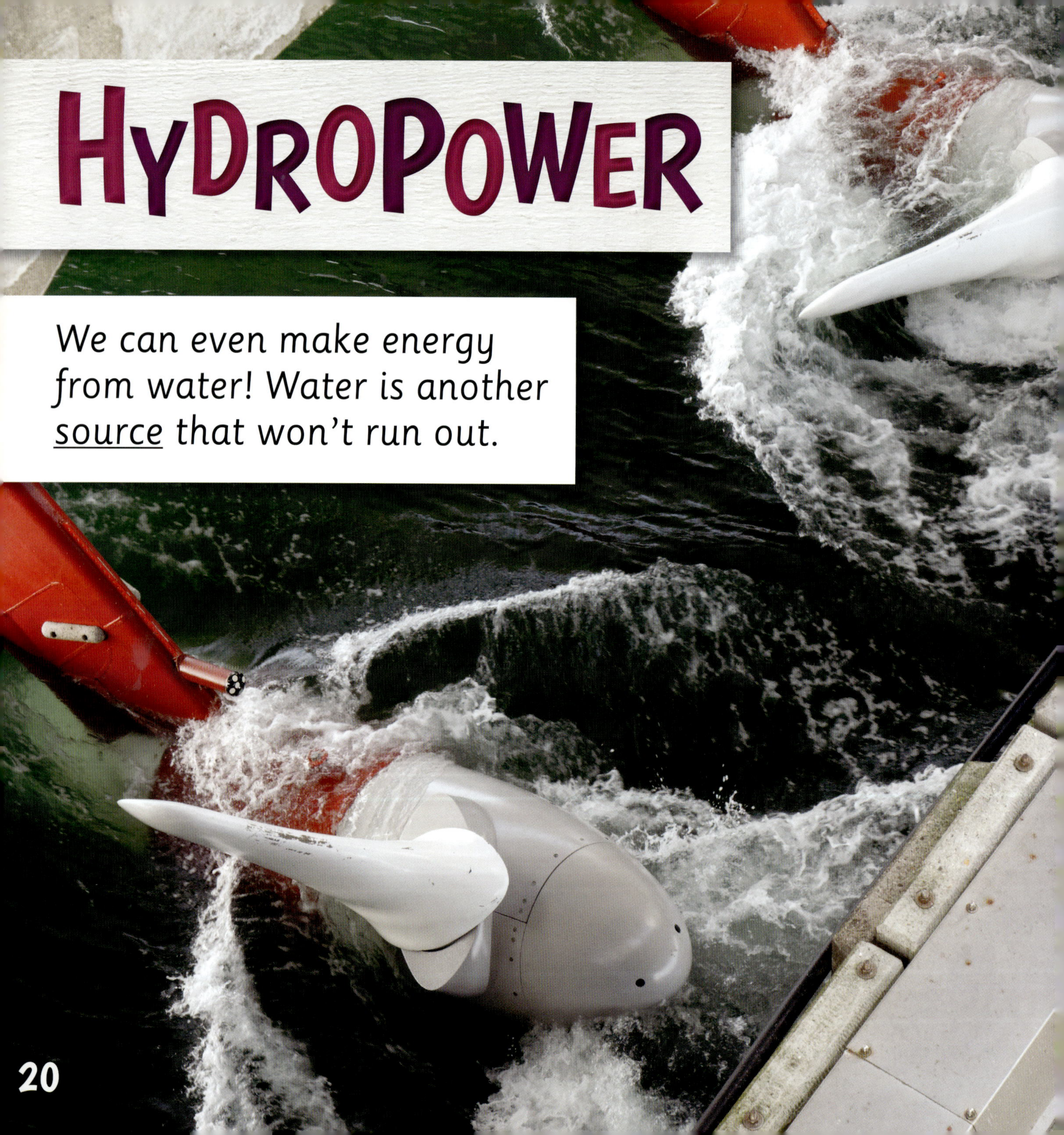

HYDROPOWER

We can even make energy from water! Water is another source that won't run out.

We can use seas, rivers and lakes to make energy.

We use dams to get power from rivers.

PROTECT THE PLANET

It's important to look after our planet.

Fossil fuels will run out. They are also bad for our planet.

We can help the planet by turning switches off at the wall, or using sources of energy that won't run out!

GLOSSARY

dams	big walls built across a river that can make energy from moving water
fuels	something that is used to make energy
natural resources	materials from the earth that can be used to make energy
renewable	can be used again and will not run out
risky	a high change of danger
source	places where something comes from

INDEX

coal 8, 12
electricity 6–7, 9–12
gas 12
home 4, 10
oil 12
planet 13, 22–23
power 4, 6, 10, 14, 16–17, 20–21
power stations 14
solar panels 17
Sun 16–17
water 20–21
wind 9, 18–19